LOW CARB HIGH FAT

Cakes and Desserts

LOW CARB HIGH FAT

Cakes and Desserts

GLUTEN~FREE AND SUGAR~FREE PIES, PASTRIES, AND MORE

Mariann Andersson

Photography by Martin Skredsvik

Translated by Gun Penhoat

Skyhorse Publishing, Inc.
New York

CONTENTS

FOREWORD

My first two baking books, *Low Carb High Fat Baking* and *Low Carb High Fat Bread*, have been lavished with high praise from many readers. I've received comments such as, "Finally some scrumptious baked goods that those of us who are gluten intolerant can enjoy" and "THANK YOU! Now I can keep eating LCHF for the rest of my life!" Even diabetics have sent me much positive feedback about my recipes—"At last, here are healthy baked goods that won't raise my blood sugar" being a frequent statement.

I have really come to understand the significant role my books have played in helping many people achieve health and well-being, and it is my sincerest wish that even more will discover that it's not only possible, but also easy, to enjoy small coffee breaks as well as more extravagant tea parties without compromising between great taste and healthy ingredients. I find it immensely gratifying to hear people tell me they've served low-carb cookies to their unsuspecting guests, who could not taste any difference between these cookies and "regular" ones. I don't think I could find a better endorsement for my recipes if I tried!

For a long time now, I've wanted to share even more delicious cookie and dessert recipes with my readers. This new book, *Low Carb High Fat Cakes and Desserts*, is therefore especially near and dear to my heart; it's chock-full of mouthwatering recipes for cakes, pies, buns, cookies, and sponge cakes—absolutely everything you could want to have on hand for a delicious coffee get-together. I hope you will try them all and will find among them many new favorites to add to your recipe collection!

— Mariann

INTRODUCTION

KEEP IN MIND

Cookies made with artificial sweeteners don't keep as long as cookies made with regular sugar (sucrose), so store them only for a few days at room temperature, or keep them in the refrigerator or the freezer instead.

Baked goods usually have better flavor if you give them time to cool down and "settle" after they've come out of the oven. A perfect example is the cinnamon buns on p. 70; they're at their loveliest a few hours after baking, or—if you can bear to wait a little longer—the day after.

An egg weighs approximately 2¼ oz (65 g). The number of servings listed for each baked good in this book is approximate. Since my recipes contain a lot of eggs, they can be quite filling. If you're serving an assortment of cookies at one time, you might want to consider cutting down on the number of servings indicated in a recipe.

To achieve a fluffier batter, whisk the eggs with a handheld electric mixer until they're light and airy (5 minutes should do the trick) before adding in the sweetener.

I always recommend using unsalted butter in my recipes. If using salted butter, however, I suggest adding just under twice the amount of sweetener indicated in the original recipe, or else the salt from the butter might come through as the dominant flavor.

Let melted butter cool before adding it to eggs, in order to avoid curdling the mixture.

Whipping cream, berries, and nuts all taste slightly sweet; if you included them in a recipe, you can decrease the amount of sweetener or even forego adding sweetener altogether. These baked goods will contain slightly more carbohydrates, but not any more than other recipes that fit within LCHF guidelines.

Baked goods containing cacao, or other bitter or sour ingredients, should be sweetened as directed by the recipe. If your taste buds are especially sensitive to bitter flavors, add some extra sweetener when using cacao.

The recommended oven temperatures in this book apply to convection ovens. If you use a conventional oven, simply increase the temperature by about 25°F. Keep a close eye on cookies the first time you try a recipe. To check for a cake's doneness, insert a toothpick near the center of the cake—it should be dry when removed.

LCHF-FRIENDLY AND NATURALLY GLUTEN-FREE "FLOURS"

Coconut flour is made from fresh coconuts. The meat is cold-pressed to separate it from the oil and water. The meat is then washed, dried, and ground into flour. It's important

to use flour made from the processed coconut fiber and not from ground coconut flakes. I use the Aman Prana brand of coconut flour because it's widely available in Sweden, as well as organic and fair-trade certified.

Coconut flour contains between 4 g and 17 g of carbohydrates per 3½ oz (100 g), depending on the brand. The amount of carbohydrates in baked goods stays low, even if the flour itself is a bit on the high side, because you only use a scant amount of it. Coconut flour is high in fiber and low in omega-6 fatty acids. This is a good thing—omega-6 fatty acids can lead to inflammation, so we should eat as few of them as possible.

½ cup (100 ml) coconut flour weighs approximately 2 oz (57 g).

You can purchase **almond flour** already ground up, but it's easy to make at home. If you prefer white flour, you'll need to blanch the almonds and rub off their skins (or you can purchase already blanched almonds). For chewier, earthier-tasting baked goods, or for foods that will be tinted by cacao or blueberries, you can leave the almond skins on.

Almond paste should be made from blanched, skinned, and freshly ground almonds, as they will impart the finest flavor. Choose the best quality almonds you can find, as musty-smelling ones are not very appetizing.

The amount of almond flour in your dough or batter can be cut by replacing some of it with coconut flour, which has lower levels of omega-6. The carbohydrate content of almond flour

varies between 4 g to 14 g per 3½ oz (100 g). However, the amount of carbohydrates in the baked goods is still small since you only use a small amount of flour.

½ cup (100 ml) almond flour weighs approximately 1¾ oz (50 g).

Hazelnut (filbert) flour is also available pre-ground, or you can grind it at home. This flour is sometimes roasted. To roast hazelnuts, set the oven to 395°F (200°C) and roast the nuts for 8 to 10 minutes. Wait for them to cool a little, and then grind them. Their carbohydrate content varies from 6.8 g to 9.4 g per 3½ oz (100 g).

½ cup (100 ml) hazelnut flour weighs approximately 1¾ oz (50 g).

*NutraFiber Flakes are fiber made from sugar beets. They're naturally gluten-free and quite absorbent. NutraFiber is sold in flake form and can be ground into flour. The flakes come in handy for bread and pie shells in which you seek a bit more chewiness or an earthier flavor. Ground into flour, NutraFiber is useful for dusting baking sheets and pans. NutraFiber Flakes contain about 5 g of carbohydrate (all of it fiber) per 8 g of product.

½ cup (100 ml) NutraFiber Flakes weighs, approximately, a little less than 1 oz (25 g).

Psyllium husk is 100 percent pulverized psyllium husk. Thanks to its high percentage of fiber (85 percent), psyllium husk will absorb a lot of liquid and thus will increase much in size. Its consistency becomes gel-like, and it holds dough together the same way gluten does; however, it can sometimes feel a bit gritty. One to two tablespoons psyllium husk is usually enough for dough. There are no carbohydrates in psyllium husk.

1 tbsp of psyllium husk weighs approximately ⅓ oz (10 g).

Oat fiber (available from Netrition.com) is very similar to Pofiber, a product composed of pure potato fiber that is unfortunately currently unavailable outside Sweden. Oat fiber has a fine texture and is lightweight. There are no carbohydrates in oat fiber.

½ cup (100 ml) oat fiber weighs approximately ⅔ oz (20 g).

CAN I SUBSTITUTE ALMOND FLOUR FOR COCONUT FLOUR, AND VICE VERSA?

Yes, substitutions will work, as long as you don't try to swap equal amounts of different flours. Coconut flour is very absorbent. You will need a lot less flour, but more liquid and eggs, than you would for almond flour.

*Instead of ½ **cup (100 ml) almond flour,** use:*
*2 tbsp coconut flour **or***
2 tbsp whole psyllium husk*

You can also mix the three flours, but you might go through a bit of trial and error before reaching the right consistency; the dough needs to be able to be worked and shaped. If you're making muffins or sponge cake, however, it can be more like a batter. Don't forget to write down the amounts so you have them handy next time you bake.

*Instead of ½ **cup (100 ml) coconut flour,** use:*
*1 cup (200 ml) almond flour and 1½ tbsp whole psyllium husk, **or***
*2 tbsp whole psyllium husk + ½ cup (100 ml) almond flour, **or***
1½ cup (300 ml) almond flour

Even here it'll be necessary to try out different amounts and combinations for best results.

SWEETENERS

Artificial sweeteners don't have the preserving quality of natural sugars such as sucrose, so they're only used in low-carbohydrate baking to add some sweetness to the food. The amount of sweetener in the recipes is merely a guideline. It is entirely up to you how much or how little you want to use.

You can select any sweetener to suit your own preference; nowadays I use a pre-made mix of erythritol and stevia, marketed in Sweden as SteviaVital®Bakery+, in all my recipes. The texture is similar to confectioner's sugar, and it's perfect for all low-carb baking. In American grocery stores, look for Truvia or generic brands of pre-mixed erythritol and stevia. To achieve the right texture, finely grind the sweetener for a few seconds in a coffee grinder or a Bullet-style grinder.

In my earlier book *Low Carb High Fat Baking*, I sweetened the food with a mix made from

3 tbsp of erythritol and ⅛ tsp of stevia powder. This mixture is still okay, but if you want to use a ready-made powder or another type of sweetener, simply check the conversion table on page 11 to find the right amount of product to use.

Erythritol is found naturally in mushrooms and some fruits, and the sweetener is made through the process of fermentation.

Stevia rebaudiana is a plant; its glucosides, which give stevia leaves their sweetness, are isolated and purified in water and alcohol. Steviol glucosides have been regularly used as a sweetener in Japan since the 1970s. In Paraguay, where the plant grows wild, native populations have used it as a sweetener for over 1,500 years. Stevia is 400 times sweeter than table sugar.

The glycemic index (GI) value of erythritol and stevia is 0, which makes them perfectly suited for diabetics. I have opted to use these sweeteners because they don't elevate blood sugar, which in turn means that they don't trigger a physiological urge for sweets, potentially leading to an overconsumption of sweet foods.

That being said, keep in mind that all sweeteners, artificial or not, can bring on cravings in people who are particularly sensitive to sweet tastes and, therefore, can cause some to overeat.

The biggest triggers of overindulgence, however, are still common table sugar (a 50-50 mix of fructose and glucose), followed by high-fructose corn syrup (HFCS), also called corn syrup, which is often found in products such as sodas, ice cream, and cookies.

All sweeteners with a GI higher than 0 raise blood sugar, so you have to be careful if you choose to use them. For someone who is addicted to sugar, even a sweetener of low to middling GI value can cause an irresistible pull toward sweet foods.

CONVERSION TABLE

2 tbsp SteviaVital®Bakery+ (eq. Truvia or generic brand) (GI 0) is the equivalent of:

3 tbsp erythritol + ¹⁄₁₆ tsp stevia (GI 0)

½ cup (100 ml) erythritol (GI 0)

½ cup (100 ml) ICA Sötströ (eq. Truvia or generic brand) (GI 0)

¼ cup (50 ml) Sukrin+ (erythritol) (GI 0)

⅛ tsp stevia powder (GI 0) - Choose a powder that is 300 to 400 times sweeter than table sugar.

½ cup (100 ml) Xylitol/birch sugar (GI 8)

½ cup (100 ml) coconut sugar (GI 35)

⅛–¼ cup (75–100 ml) agave syrup (GI 50)

¼ cup (50 ml) honey (GI 70)

½ cup (100 ml) cane sugar (GI 97)

½ cup (100 ml) table sugar (GI 97)

DO YOU WANT TO BAKE WITHOUT DAIRY PRODUCTS?

You can easily swap out dairy for several other options in most of the recipes in this book. You can use coconut fat instead of butter, but make

sure that it's a neutral-tasting, or flavorless, variety. Use any liquid instead of whipping cream, crème fraîche, and cream cheese, as long as the quantity stays the same. Another good substitute for regular dairy is the popular LCHF "egg milk," a whisked mixture of coconut fat, water, and egg.

SMART TIPS!

All "squares" can be baked in a round, 8½" (22 cm) wide spring-form pan, and all round cakes can also be baked in a rectangular 6" × 10" (15 × 25 cm) pan.

The nut cookies on p. 84 are perfect to make when you have a lot of leftover egg whites to use up, which often happens when you cook and bake according to LCHF guidelines.

Remember that you can also freeze egg whites.

Always line the bottom of a springform pan with parchment paper to make sure that cake batter doesn't stick to the bottom while it bakes. It's a good idea to line the sides of the pan as well to ensure that the cake doesn't stick there either. I always line the pan when baking a sponge cake in a loaf pan. Just press the parchment paper down and make some folds in the corners. Good quality parchment paper can be reused several times.

Gluten-free flour tends to produce crumbly dough. The best way to deal with this is to wet your hands and baking tools, and press the dough gently together with your fingers. The same rule applies if the dough is sticky—use wet hands and tools.

Cakes and Pies

Queen Cake

A delicious cake that is sure to be a crowd pleaser, not to mention a great way to use local berries when they're in season.

SERVES **14–18**

CAKE

¼ cup (50 g) unsalted butter
7 large eggs
½ cup (100 ml) whipping cream
2 tbsp erythritol/stevia blend (or
  other sweetener of your choice,
  see page 11)
⅔ cup (150 ml) coconut flour
2 tbsp whole psyllium husk,
  unflavored
½ tsp vanilla powder, or
  1 tsp vanilla extract
2 tsp baking powder

BLUEBERRY MOUSSE

4 sheets of gelatin, or equivalent
  amount gelatin powder
7 oz (200 g) blueberries, frozen
1½ tbsp erythritol/stevia blend
  (or other sweetener of your
  choice, see page 11)
3½ oz (100 g) mascarpone, or
  other cream cheese
1 cup (200 ml) whipping cream

RASPBERRY MOUSSE

4 sheets of gelatin, or equivalent
  amount gelatin powder
7 oz (200 g) raspberries, frozen
1½ tbsp erythritol/stevia blend
  (or other sweetener of your
  choice, see page 11)
3½ oz mascarpone, or other
  cream cheese
1 cup (200 ml) whipping cream

GARNISH

1⅓–1¾ cup (350–400 ml)
  whipping cream
Fresh raspberries and blueberries

Directions: Preheat the oven to 350°F (175°C). Line the bottom of an 8½" to 9½" (22–24 cm) springform pan with parchment paper. Melt the butter and let it cool.

Cake: Beat the eggs for at least 5 minutes, until pale and fluffy. Add in the cooled butter, followed by the whipping cream.

Mix the dry ingredients thoroughly and incorporate them into the batter; pour the batter into the prepared springform pan.

Set the cake on the middle rack of the oven, and bake for approximately 25 minutes.

Let the cake cool completely before slicing it into 3 equal, horizontal layers (it'll be easier to cut layers if you bake the cake in the smaller, 8½-inch springform pan). The layers of cake can be frozen with parchment paper placed between the layers, and used cold or partly defrosted.

Mousse: Soak the sheets of gelatin in cold water for at least 5 minutes; if using gelatin powder, follow the directions on the packet carefully, as different brands of gelatin can have different consistencies. In a saucepan, bring the frozen berries to a boil, and cook for 2 minutes until they soften and become liquid. Press the berries through a sieve to make a purée. Mix half the purée with

the sweetener and mascarpone or cream cheese.

In a saucepan, heat the remainder of the purée; stir in the gelatin. Let cool, then mix in the berry and mascarpone mixture.

Beat the whipping cream until soft peaks form, then fold it into the gelatin mixture. Chill this mousse so it sets before adding it to the cake layers.

Assembly: Place the bottom layer of the cake in a (now clean and dry) springform pan. Spread the layer evenly with blueberry mousse—make sure to pack it down.

Place the next layer of cake on top of the blueberry mousse, and press it down gently. Spread the second layer with raspberry mousse, again carefully packing the mousse. Invert the last layer of cake, and set it topside down onto the raspberry mousse. Make sure the surface is flat.

Wrap the cake in plastic wrap, and leave it overnight in the refrigerator or freezer. If you choose to freeze the cake, you'll need to defrost it in the refrigerator for 8 to 10 hours before serving.

Whip the cream and spread it evenly over the entire cake. Pipe a decorative edge around the top of the cake, and place a mound of fresh raspberries and blueberries at its center.

Black Currant and White Chocolate Mousse Cake

Black currants and white chocolate make a fine pair in this cake.

SERVES 14–18

CAKE

½ cup (100 g) unsalted butter
7 large eggs
½ cup (100 ml) water
½ cup (100 ml) coconut flour
1 tbsp psyllium husk
½ tsp vanilla powder, or 1 tsp vanilla extract
2 tsp baking powder
2 tbsp erythritol/stevia blend (or other sweetener of your choice, see page 11)
¼ cup (50 ml) cacao powder

BLACK CURRANT JUICE

17½ oz (500 g) black currants, fresh or frozen
½ cup (100 ml) water
1½ tbsp erythritol/stevia blend (or other sweetener of your choice, see page 11)

BLACK CURRANT MOUSSE

3 sheets of gelatin, or equivalent amount gelatin powder
Approx. ½ cup (100 ml) black currant juice
3½ oz (100 g) mascarpone, or cream cheese
½ tsp vanilla powder, or 1 tsp vanilla extract
1 tbsp erythritol/stevia blend (or other sweetener of your choice, see page 11)
1 cup (200 ml) whipping cream

WHITE CHOCOLATE MOUSSE

1½ cup (300 ml) whipping cream
¼ cup cocoa butter (50 g) or 3½ oz (100 g) white chocolate, sweetened with stevia
2 large egg yolks, at room temperature
1½ tbsp erythritol/stevia blend (or other sweetener of your choice, see page 11)
½ tsp vanilla extract (can be omitted if you're using white chocolate)

BLACK CURRANT JELLY FROSTING

2 sheets of gelatin, or equivalent amount gelatin powder
½ cup (100 ml) black currant juice
¼ cup (50 ml) water
1 tbsp erythritol/stevia blend (or other sweetener of your choice, see page 11)

GARNISH

2 cups (400 ml) whipping cream

Directions: Preheat the oven to 350°F (175°C). Line the bottom of an 8½" to 9½" (22–24 cm) springform pan with parchment paper. Melt the butter and let it cool.

Cake: Beat the eggs for at least 5 minutes, until light and fluffy. Add in the butter, followed by the water.

Mix the dry ingredients thoroughly and incorporate them into the batter. Pour the batter into the prepared springform pan, and bake it on the oven's middle rack for approximately 30 minutes.

Let the cake cool completely before cutting it into 3 horizontal layers (it'll be easier to cut the layers if you choose to bake the cake in the smaller, 8½-inch springform pan). The layers of cake can be frozen with parchment paper set between the layers, and then used cold or partly defrosted.

Black currant juice: Bring black currants, water, and sweetener to a boil in a saucepan, and let simmer until the berries are soft, about 5 minutes. Press the berries through a sieve to collect the juice. You can freeze the juice if you're not going to be using it immediately.

Black currant mousse: Soak the sheets of gelatin in cold water for at least 5 minutes; if using powdered gelatin, follow the directions on the packet. Warm up ½ cup (100 ml) of the black currant juice, and dissolve the gelatin in the warm juice. Let cool slightly.

Whip the mascarpone with vanilla powder or vanilla extract and sweetener until soft peaks form.

Stir in the cooling black currant/gelatin juice into the mascarpone mixture. Add the whipped cream and mix thoroughly.

White chocolate mousse: Whip the cream until soft peaks form.

In a bowl set over a warm water bath (bain-marie) gently melt the cacao butter. Remove the bowl from the heat and whisk in the egg yolks, sweetener, and vanilla extract. Add the whipped cream and mix thoroughly; mixing will be easier if the melted cacao butter and the whipped cream are at room temperature.

Black currant jelly frosting: Soak the sheets of gelatin in cold water for at least 5 minutes; if using gelatin powder, follow the directions on the packet.

Warm up ½ cup (100 ml) of the black currant juice, and dissolve the gelatin in the warm juice. Let cool.

Assembly: Set the bottom layer of the cake in the (now washed and dry) springform pan. Spread some black currant mousse in an even layer, and make sure to pack the mousse down into a solid layer. Place the second layer of cake onto the black currant mousse, and gently press it down. Spread the chocolate mousse on top, packing this layer as well. Invert the last layer of cake and place it topside down onto the chocolate mousse. Make sure the surface is flat and even.

Wrap the cake in plastic wrap and place it in the refrigerator overnight, or freeze it. If the cake is frozen, remove it from the freezer and defrost it in the refrigerator for 8 to 10 hours before serving.

Garnish: Whip the cream and spread it evenly over the entire cake. Pipe a decorative edge around the top of the cake. Pipe the edge high enough to keep the black currant jelly frosting in place. Pour the cooled black currant gelatin juice inside the piped cream edging, and chill the cake until the jelly has set into a glossy top. Pipe the rest of the cream in a lattice (or other) pattern over the top of the cake.

I prefer to make my own white chocolate from cacao butter. However, if you can find a premium-quality white chocolate sweetened with stevia, it will work just as well. You'll need 3½ oz (100 g) of it.

Tips! *The cake will be larger in diameter and not as tall if you bake it in the larger, 8½" to 9½" (22–24 cm) springform pan, but you can still get 2 or 3 layers out of it. You can freeze the leftover egg whites. Lemon curd makes an excellent filling in cakes and baked goods containing berries. It is also scrumptious when simply smeared on toast.*

Lemon Curd Layer Cake

Do you love all things lemon? If so, this layer cake will soon become a favorite!

SERVES **12–14**

CAKE

7 large eggs

½ cup (100 ml) water

Grated rind from 1 organic lemon

3 tbsp erythritol/stevia blend (or other sweetener of your choice, see page 11)

½ cup (100 ml) coconut flour

1 tbsp whole, unflavored psyllium husk

½ tsp vanilla powder, or 1 tsp vanilla extract

1 tsp baking powder

LEMON CURD (MAKES APPROX. 600 ML)

4 large eggs

4 egg yolks

6 tbsp erythritol/stevia blend (or other sweetener of your choice, see page 11)

Grated rind from 4 organic lemons

Lemon juice from 4 organic lemons, approx. 1 cup (200 ml)

¾ cup (200 g) unsalted butter, softened

GARNISH

½ cup (100 ml) lemon curd

1½ cup (300 ml) whipping cream

Directions: Preheat the oven to 350°F (175°C). Line the bottom of a 6" (15 cm) round baking pan with parchment paper, and butter the sides. Line the side of the pan with parchment paper, making the paper extend 2" over the top of the side.

Cake: Beat the eggs for 5 minutes until light and fluffy. Add the water and grated lemon rind; mix thoroughly.

Pour the batter into the prepared baking pan, and bake on the middle rack of the oven for approximately 40 minutes.

Let the cake cool completely before you slice it into 4 or 5 horizontal layers. The layers can be frozen with parchment set between the layers. The layers can be used cold or partly defrosted.

Lemon curd: In a saucepan with a heavy bottom, whisk together eggs, egg yolks, and sweetener. Add the grated lemon rind and lemon juice, and continue whisking.

Heat the curd gently while whisking. DO NOT LET IT COME TO A BOIL. Heat the mixture until it thickens, then remove the saucepan from the heat and stir in the softened butter.

Pour the curd into a clean glass jar if you are not going to use it immediately. It will keep for a few days in the refrigerator, or it can be frozen in small portions with excellent results.

Lemon cream: Whip ½ cup (100 ml) lemon curd with the whipping cream until thick and of a spreadable consistency.

Assembly: Set one layer of cake on a cake platter. Spread it with some lemon curd, and set the next layer of cake on top. Repeat these steps with the remaining layers of cake and the lemon curd, finishing by inverting the last layer and setting it topside down onto the lemon curd.

Spread lemon cream over the entire cake. Using a star attachment, pipe small stars onto the cake for decoration.

Chocolate Coconut Cake with Coconut Mousse and Black Currant Jelly Frosting

Not only does this cake look luxurious and delicate, it tastes so, too!

SERVES 8–10

CAKE
3½ oz (100 g) dark chocolate
 (preferably 90% cacao)
¼ cup (50 g) unsalted butter
1 egg yolk
1 tbsp coconut flour
1 tbsp erythritol/stevia blend (or
 other sweetener of your choice,
 see page 11), optional

COCONUT MOUSSE
1 cup (200 ml) crème fraîche
 or sour cream
1½ tbsp erythritol/stevia blend
 (or other sweetener of your choice,
 see page 11)
1 cup (200 ml) grated and unsweetened coconut
1 cup (200 ml) whipping cream

BLACK CURRANT JELLY FROSTING
1 cup (200 ml) black currants (or
 same amount black currant juice -
 see page 16 for the recipe)
1½ tbsp erythritol/stevia blend (or
 other sweetener of your choice,
 see page 11)
¼ cup (50 ml) water
2½ sheets of gelatin, or equivalent
 amount in powder

GARNISH
Black currants

Directions: Make the coconut mousse one day ahead. Preheat the oven to 350°F (175°C). Line the bottom of an 8" to 9" (21–22 cm) springform pan with parchment paper.

Coconut mousse: Whip the crème fraîche with sweetener until thick. Stir in the grated coconut; set in the refrigerator and chill overnight.

Cake: Melt the chocolate and butter; stir in the egg yolk, sweetener, and coconut flour.

 Spread the batter over the bottom of the prepared spring-form pan and bake for 5 minutes on the middle rack of the preheated oven. Let this layer cool completely.

Black currant jelly frosting: Set aside a few currants for the garnish. Bring black currants, sweetener, and water to a boil. Simmer until the berries give up their juice, and then pass the liquid through a sieve.

 Soak the sheets of gelatin in cold water for approximately 5 minutes; if using gelatin powder, follow the directions on the packet.

 Warm up ¼ cup (50 ml) of the black currant juice, and dissolve the gelatin in the warm juice. Mix it with the rest of the black currant juice, and let cool.

Assembly: Start with the coconut mousse and the layer of chocolate cake. Whip the cream until stiff peaks form. Mix it into the mousse. Spread the mousse over the chocolate layer, and make sure the layer is as flat and smooth as possible. Let the cake chill in the refrigerator for a while.

 With the sides of the springform pan still in place, spread the black currant jelly over the top of the cake and chill the cake until the jellied "gloss" has set completely. Run a sharp, warm knife around the edge of the cake in the springform pan prior to serving. The leftover black currants make a nice garnish.

Tips! Strawberries work well here, too! The coconut mousse is versatile and makes excellent layers for other types of cakes as well.

Blueberry Mousse Cake

Do you want your dessert to dazzle both in presentation and flavor? If so, this cake is a good choice for your next gathering! The cake is, naturally, just as delectable when made with raspberries or with strawberries.

SERVES 8–10

CAKE

⅛ cup (25 g) unsalted butter
2 large eggs
2 tbsp water
1 tbsp erythritol/stevia blend
   (or other sweetener of your
   choice, see page 11)
¼ cup (50 ml) coconut flour
¼ cup (50 ml) almond flour or
   ¼ cup (25 g) ground
   almonds
¼ tsp vanilla powder or ½ tsp
   vanilla extract
½ tsp baking powder
Grated rind of one organic lemon
oat fiber or coconut flour, for
   dusting the baking pan

BLUEBERRY MOUSSE

8 sheets of gelatin, or equivalent
   amount in powder form
1 vanilla bean or 1 tsp vanilla
   extract
14 oz (400 g) blueberries, fresh
   or frozen
2½ tbsp erythritol/stevia blend
   (or other sweetener of your
   choice, see page 11)
2½ cup (500 ml) whipping cream
1½ cup (300 ml) crème fraîche

GARNISH

Fresh blueberries

Directions: Preheat the oven to 350°F (175°C). Melt the butter and let cool. Line the bottom of a small, 6" (15 cm) springform pan with parchment paper. Butter the sides of the pan and dust with oat fiber or coconut flour.

Cake: Beat the eggs for 5 minutes until light and airy. Add in the melted butter and water. Mix the dry ingredients thoroughly, and stir into the batter. Pour the batter into the prepared pan. Bake on the middle rack of the oven for about 12 minutes. Let the cake cool completely on a rack.

Blueberry mousse: Soak the sheets of gelatin in cold water for 5 minutes; if using gelatin powder, follow the instructions on the packet carefully. Scrape out the vanilla seeds from the pod if you're using a vanilla bean. Warm the blueberries, vanilla, and sweetener until the berries give off their juice. If you want a smoother mousse, blend or press the berries through a sieve.

Dissolve the gelatin in the warm berries and let the mix cool for a while. Stir the crème fraîche into the blueberries. Whip the whipping cream in a separate bowl until firm, and then add it to the berry/gelatin mixture.

Assembly: Place a fresh piece of parchment paper at the bottom of the baking pan, and line the sides with parchment paper to a height of approximately 6" (15 cm).

Return the cake to the baking pan. If you want the mousse to cover the sides of this layer, too, you'll have to cut away ½" (1 cm) all around the edge of the cake.

Spread approximately ¼ of the blueberry mousse onto the cake. Shake the pan carefully, and then gently tap it against the work surface to get rid of any air pockets. Pour in the rest of the mousse and, once again, tap the pan against the work surface until the mousse is evenly distributed. Smooth the surface of the mousse. Cover the pan with plastic wrap, and place the cake in the refrigerator overnight. You can also put the cake in the freezer, and remove it about 30 minutes before serving. If the cake has been stored in the freezer for several days, it will need to be removed and defrosted in the refrigerator for 10 to 12 hours prior to serving. Remove the plastic wrap while the cake is still frozen, but make sure that the cake has had time to thaw a little before removing the sides of the springform pan. Remove the parchment paper and even out the sides and top if necessary.

Garnish with fresh blueberries right before serving.

Tips! You can double the
ingredients for the cake to
make a cake measuring
8½" to 9½" (22–24 cm)
in diameter.

Almond Cake with Champagne and Strawberry Mousse

SERVES 12–14

CAKE

Oat fiber or coconut flour, for dusting

2 large eggs

2 tbsp erythritol/stevia blend
(or other sweetener of your choice,
see page 11)

2 tbsp cacao

10½ oz (300 g) ground almonds

STRAWBERRY MOUSSE

4 sheets of gelatin, or equivalent
amount in powder form

6¼ oz (175 g) fresh strawberries,
or if using frozen, defrosted

5¼ oz (150 g) fresh strawberries,
coarsely chopped

1½ tbsp erythritol/stevia blend
(or other sweetener of your
choice, see page 11)

1½ cup (300 ml) whipping cream

CHAMPAGNE MOUSSE

7 sheets of gelatin, or equivalent
amount in powder form

1¼ cup (250 ml) whipping cream

8¾ oz (250 g) mascarpone

3 tbsp erythritol/stevia blend
(or other sweetener of your choice,
see page 11)

2 egg yolks

¼ cup (50 ml) water

1 cup (200 ml) dry champagne, or
dry white wine

GARNISH

7 oz (200 g) fresh strawberries

Directions: Preheat the oven to 350°F (175°C). Line the bottom of an 8½" (22 cm) springform pan with parchment paper. Butter the sides of the pan, and dust them with oat fiber or coconut flour.

Cake: Beat the eggs until light and fluffy. Add in sweetener and cacao; stir in the ground almonds.

Pour the batter into the prepared pan and bake on the lower rack of the oven for 10 to 15 minutes. Let the cake cool, and then loosen it from the pan.

Strawberry mousse: Soak the sheets of gelatin in cold water for 5 minutes. If using gelatin powder, follow the instructions on the packet, carefully.

Mix 6¼ oz (175 g) strawberries with the sweetener until you have a purée. Warm ¼ cup (50 ml) of this purée, and dissolve the gelatin in it. Add in the remainder of the purée and let the mix cool down a little. Stir in the 5¼ oz (150 g) coarsely chopped strawberries. Whip the cream and stir it into the strawberry gelatin. Mix thoroughly and place the mousse in the refrigerator to set further.

Champagne mousse: Soak the sheets of gelatin in cold water for 5 minutes. If using gelatin powder, follow the instructions on the packet. Whip the cream until firm.

Whip together mascarpone, sweetener, and egg yolks; stir in the champagne. Warm ¼ cup (50 ml) water and dissolve the gelatin in it. Let it cool down a bit. Whisk the mascarpone mixture into the gelatin, and then incorporate the whipped cream. Place the mousse in the refrigerator.

Assembly: Place a fresh piece of parchment paper in the bottom of the springform pan, and line the sides of the pan with strips of parchment paper, approximately an inch taller than the top of the sides. Return the cake to the pan.

Spread the strawberry mousse evenly over the cake, and shake the pan gently, then tap it gently on the work surface to get rid of any air bubbles in the mousse. Chill the cake for another 30 minutes if the mousse doesn't look fully set.

Spread a layer of champagne mousse over the strawberry mousse, and repeat the gentle shaking and tapping to remove air bubbles and to make the mousse spread evenly. Even out the surface.

Cover the cake with plastic wrap and let the cake sit for at least 6 hours—but preferably overnight—in the refrigerator.

Garnish the cake with fresh strawberries, and perhaps some fresh lemon balm, right before serving.

Frozen Chocolate Mousse Cake

Ice cream cake is a beloved dessert to many, so why not offer your guests a frozen chocolate mousse cake laced with coffee at your next gathering? Omit the coffee, and the cake makes a great treat for a children's party, too!

SERVES 8–10

CAKE

2 large eggs
2 cups (200 g) almonds, ground
2 bitter almonds, finely ground, or
 1 tsp almond extract
¼ cup (50 ml) coconut flour
1–2 tbsp cacao powder
1½ tbsp erythritol/stevia blend
 (or other sweetener of your choice,
 see page 11)

FROSTING

5¼ (150 g) dark chocolate, 90%
 cacao
3 egg yolks
½ tbsp instant coffee granules
 (optional)
1 tbsp hot water
1 tbsp erythritol/stevia blend (or
 other sweetener of your choice,
 see page 11)
2 cups (400 ml) whipping cream

GARNISH

Grated chocolate
Roasted, slivered almonds

Directions: Preheat the oven to 350° F (175° C). Line the bottom of an 8" (21–22 cm) springform pan with parchment paper.

Cake: Beat the eggs lightly. Mix the dry ingredients thoroughly and stir in the eggs. Spread the batter in the springform pan, and bake on the middle rack of the oven for about 10 minutes. Let cool completely.

Frosting: Melt the chocolate over a bowl of simmering water (bain-marie). Let it cool a little. Incorporate the yolks, one at a time, into the cooled chocolate.

Dissolve the coffee granules in the hot water. Mix the coffee and sweetener into the chocolate mixture.

Whip the cream until it's thick and voluminous, and fold it carefully into the chocolate/coffee mixture. Mix to achieve a smooth blend.

Spread the chocolate mousse over the cooled layer of cake. Place the cake in the freezer for approximately 5 hours.

To serve: Serve the cake partly thawed. Set it, covered, to defrost in the refrigerator for 45 minutes, and then at room temperature for 15 minutes.

Right before serving, decorate the cake with some grated chocolate and/or roasted, slivered almonds. You can also melt some dark chocolate and spread it in a thin layer on a sheet of parchment paper. Let the chocolate set (it will harden). Cut or break off thin pieces of chocolate to use as a garnish.

Sumptuous Rhubarb Pie

Serve this pie with lightly whipped cream or vanilla custard, or simply by itself as it comes out of the oven. Whichever way you choose, it is absolutely delicious.

SERVES 10–12

PIE CRUST

¾ cup (200 g) unsalted butter

3 large eggs

1–2 tbsp erythritol/stevia blend (or other sweetener of your choice, see page 11)

½ cup (100 ml) coconut flour

½ cup (100 ml) almond flour or 1¾ oz (50 g) ground almonds

2 tsp baking powder

½ tsp vanilla powder or 1 tsp vanilla extract

FILLING

14 oz (400 g) rhubarb

2 cups (400 ml) almond flour or 7 oz (200 g) ground almonds

1–2 bitter almonds, ground, or 1 tsp almond extract

1½–2 tbsp erythritol/stevia blend (or other sweetener of your choice, see page 11)

1 tbsp whipping cream

2 large eggs

⅔ cup (150 g) unsalted butter, softened

Directions: Preheat the oven to 350°F (175°C). Melt the butter and let it cool.

Pie crust: Beat the eggs until light and airy, about 5 minutes. Add in the melted cool butter.

Mix the dry ingredients thoroughly, and incorporate well into the egg batter.

Line a pie pan with ¾ of the pastry, extending the pastry about ½"– 1" (1½–2 cm) up the sides of the pan.

Filling: Clean and chop the rhubarb into ½" (1 cm) chunks.

Mix the almond flour with the ground bitter almonds or almond extract and sweetener; add in the whipping cream. While mixing, add in the eggs, then the butter. Stir in half the chunks of rhubarb. Spread the filling over the crust, and cover with the rest of the rhubarb; save the prettier pink chunks for the top.

Roll out the rest of the dough and cut it into narrow strips. Place the strips in a lattice pattern over the top of the pie filling.

Bake the pie on the middle rack of the oven for 20 to 25 minutes. The Mazarin almond filling should be almost set when coming out of the oven but will set further as the pie cools.

Raspberry Panna Cotta Pie

Wonderful raspberry pie! It's truly a dream dessert to serve at one of summer's many cookouts.

SERVES 8–10

PIE CRUST
½ cup (125 g) unsalted butter

3 large eggs

1½ tbsp erythritol/stevia blend (or other sweetener of your choice, see page 11)

¾ cup (150 ml) coconut flour

¾ cup (150 ml) almonds, finely chopped (or slivered almonds)

2 tsp baking powder

½ tsp vanilla powder or 1 tsp vanilla extract

Slivered almonds for the baking pan

RASPBERRY PANNA COTTA
4 sheets of gelatin, or equivalent amount of gelatin powder

1 cup (200 ml) whipping cream

1 cup (200 ml) crème fraîche

1½ tbsp erythritol/stevia blend (or other sweetener of your choice, see page 11)

8¾ oz (250 g) raspberries; if using frozen, thawed

GARNISH
Fresh raspberries

Directions: Preheat the oven to 350°F (175°C). Melt the butter and let it cool. Line the bottom of an 8½" to 9½" (22–24 cm) springform pan with parchment paper. Butter and cover the pan with slivered almonds, at least 1¼" (3 cm) up the sides.

Pie crust: Beat the eggs until light and fluffy, and then add in the cooled butter.

Mix the dry ingredients thoroughly, and incorporate them in the batter to make a dough.
Press the dough into the prepared pan.

Bake on the middle rack of the oven for about 10 minutes. Let cool.

Raspberry panna cotta: Soak the sheets of gelatin in cold water for 5 minutes; if using gelatin powder, follow the instructions on the packet.

Place whipping cream, crème fraîche, and sweetener in a saucepan, stir, heat, and let simmer until the sweetener is dissolved. Squeeze out the water from the gelatin. Remove the saucepan from the heat, and mix the gelatin in with the cream mixture. Let it cool.

Purée the raspberries, and fold the purée into the cooled cream mixture.

Pour the panna cotta into the pie crust. Place the pie in the refrigerator, and let it sit for at least 3 hours or until the panna cotta has set.

Garnish the panna cotta pie with fresh raspberries. A dollop of lightly whipped cream pairs well with this, so why not pipe some whipped cream onto each slice?

Tips! *The pie crust can be frozen. If you don't have raspberries, straw-berries and blueberries make fine substitutions.*

Coconut Pie

A delicious pie that is sure to be a hit with coconut lovers!

SERVES **10–12**

PIE CRUST

½ cup (100 g) unsalted butter

2 large eggs

½ cup (100 ml) coconut flour

½ cup (100 ml) grated, unsweetened
  coconut

1 tbsp erythritol/stevia blend (or
  other sweetener of your choice, see
  page 11)

1 tsp baking powder

Grated, unsweetened coconut for the
  pan

FILLING

1 sheet of gelatin or equivalent
  amount of gelatin powder

1½ cup (300 ml) whipping cream

½ cup (100 ml) water

1½ tbsp erythritol/stevia blend (or
  other sweetener of your choice, see
  page 11)

½ tsp vanilla powder or 1 tsp vanilla
  extract

2½ cups (500 ml) unsweetened
  coconut flakes

2 large eggs

⅓ cup (100 g) unsalted butter

GARNISH

¼–½ cup (50 ml–100 ml) grated,
  unsweetened coconut

1 cup (200 ml) whipped cream

Directions: Preheat the oven to 350°F
(175°C). Line the bottom of an 8" to 9"
(21–22 cm) round pie pan with a sheet of
parchment paper. Butter the pan and scatter
grated coconut over the bottom and at least
1" (2 cm) up the sides of the pan. Melt the
butter and let it cool.

Pie crust: Beat the eggs until light and fluffy.
Add in the melted and cooled butter. Mix all
the dry ingredients thoroughly and incorporate them into the batter to make a dough.

Press the dough into the pie pan and up
the sides. Chill the dough for 30 minutes
to stop the pie crust from shrinking while
baking.

Bake on the middle rack of the oven for
approximately 10 minutes.

Filling: Soak the sheet of gelatin in cold water
for at least 5 minutes; if using gelatin powder, follow the instructions on the packet.

Bring whipping cream, water, sweetener,
and vanilla to a boil. Whisk in the coconut
flakes and the eggs, and let simmer until
mixture starts to thicken. Fold in the gelatin
and then the butter. Let it cool.

Spread the filling in the pie crust, and set
the pie in the refrigerator for several hours.

Garnish: Toast grated coconut in a hot frying
pan until it takes on a light color. Let cool.
Pipe the whipped cream onto the pie, and
right before serving, sprinkle the pie with the
toasted coconut.

Tips! *Place the spring-form pan on a baking sheet to keep things clean, as butter might leak while baking.*

Rhubarb Cheesecake

These days you can find rhubarb in the freezer section of most supermarkets, making this delectable cheesecake a delicacy you can enjoy year-round.

SERVES **10–12**

PIE CRUST

¾ cup (200 g) unsalted butter

3 large eggs

2 tbsp erythritol/stevia blend (or other sweetener of your choice, see page 11)

2½ cups (500 ml) almond flour or 2⅔ cup (250 g) ground almonds

½ cup (100 ml) NutraFiber flakes, ground to powder (ground measure)

¼ cup (50 ml) coconut flour

1 tbsp whole, unflavored psyllium husk

¼ tsp vanilla powder or ½ tsp vanilla extract

RHUBARB COMPÔTE

14 oz (400 g) rhubarb

2 tbsp erythritol/stevia blend (or other sweetener of your choice, see page 11)

FILLING

1 vanilla bean or 1 tsp vanilla extract

17½ oz (500 g) cream cheese

8¾ oz quark, preferably 10% (can be substituted with cottage cheese or farmer's cheese)

2 tbsp erythritol/stevia blend (or other sweetener of your choice, see page 11)

3 tbsp coconut flour

4 large eggs

¼ cup (100 ml) whipping cream

¼ cup (50 g) cacao butter

3½ oz (100 g) white chocolate

Directions: Preheat the oven to 350°F (175°C). Line the bottom and sides of an 8" (22 cm) pie pan with parchment paper. Melt and cool the butter.

Pie crust: Beat the eggs until light and fluffy, and mix in the melted and cooled butter. Mix all dry ingredients thoroughly, and stir them into the batter to make dough. Let the dough rest for 5 minutes.

Press the dough into the pie plate and up the sides. Chill for 30 minutes to stop the dough from shrinking while baking.

Prebake the piecrust on the middle rack of the oven for 10 minutes. Remove the pie pan from the oven and lower the oven temperature to 300°F (150°C).

Rhubarb compôte: Chop the rhubarb into ½" chunks. Bring them to a boil together with the sweetener. Let the rhubarb soften on low heat until it has given off its juice, leaving a few pieces intact.

Filling: Add the vanilla extract, or scrape out the vanilla seeds from the pod if you're using a vanilla bean. Beat the cream cheese, quark, vanilla, sweetener, and coconut flour until it's creamy and without lumps. Beat in the eggs, one at a time. Add in the whipping cream and continue beating.

Melt the cacao butter carefully in a bowl over a water bath (bain-marie).

Gently add the cacao butter to the batter. Stir in the rhubarb compôte, a bit unevenly. Pour the filling into the prebaked piecrust.

Return the pie to the middle rack of the oven for another 1½ hours. Let it cool in the oven, preferably overnight.

Serve the pie at room temperature or chilled.

Strawberry Mousse Mini Pies with Lime Jelly Topping

Only two words can describe these morsels of perfection—heavenly and unforgettable!

MAKES **4** MINIATURE PIES

ALMOND CRUST

⅓ cup (75 g) unsalted butter, softened

1½ tbsp erythritol/stevia blend (or other sweetener of your choice, see page 11)

1 large egg

½ cup (100 ml) almond flour or ½ cup (50 g) ground almonds

1 bitter almond, ground, or ½ tsp almond extract

¼ cup (50 ml) coconut flour

STRAWBERRY MOUSSE

1 sheet of gelatin or equivalent amount of powder

4½ oz strawberries, fresh or frozen

1 tbsp erythritol/stevia blend (or other sweetener of your choice, see page 11)

⅓ vanilla bean, seeds only, or 1 tsp vanilla extract

1 oz (30 g) mascarpone or cream cheese

¾ cup (150 ml) whipping cream

TOPPING

Sliced fresh strawberries

LIME JELLY

2 sheets of gelatin, or equivalent amount gelatin powder

½ cup (100 ml) water

2 tbsp erythritol/stevia blend (or other sweetener of your choice, see page 11)

¼ cup (50 ml) juice from 2 or 3 organic limes + peel

Directions: Preheat the oven to 350°F (175°C).

Almond crust: Cream the butter and sweetener; add in the egg and stir some more. Mix the dry ingredients thoroughly, and incorporate them to make dough.

Press the dough into the bottom and up the sides of four 4" × 2" (10 × 5 cm), miniature pie pans. Chill for at least 30 minutes to stop the dough from shrinking while baking.

Bake the pies on the middle rack of the oven for approximately 12 minutes. Cool, and store them in the refrigerator.

Strawberry mousse: Soak the sheets of gelatin in cold water for at least 5 minutes; if using gelatin powder, follow the instructions on the packet.

Heat strawberries, sweetener, and the seeds from the vanilla bean; add some water to the pan if needed. Keep heating until the strawberries become relatively mushy.

Incorporate the gelatin into the strawberry mush. Add in the mascarpone and mix well.

Whip the cream until soft peaks form, and fold it into the mousse.

Fill the chilled pie crusts with the strawberry mousse. Pile plenty of sliced strawberries on top. Store the pies in a cool place.

Lime jelly: Soak the sheets of gelatin in cold water for at least 5 minutes.

Heat the water with sweetener and the juice and rind from the limes. Sieve out the rind.

Stir the gelatin into the warm lime juice. Chill until the jelly starts setting, and then drizzle the jelly over the sliced strawberries. If the jelly sets too quickly, warm it gently and start over.

Store the miniature pies in a cool place until it's time to serve them.

Sponge Cakes,
Muffins,
and Sheet Cakes

Sponge Cake with Various Flavors

A delicious sponge cake isn't just something you can enjoy on sunny days—it's a welcome treat anytime and everywhere. Serve it up with a cup of coffee, and try it out with the various flavors I've suggested here.

SERVES 12–14

½ cup (100 g) unsalted butter

5 large eggs

1 cup (200 ml) crème fraîche or sour cream

2 tbsp erythritol/stevia blend (or other sweetener of your choice, see page 11)

1 tsp vanilla powder or 1 tsp vanilla extract

½ cup (100 ml) almond flour or ½ cup (50 g) ground almonds

½ cup (100 ml) coconut flour

1 heaping tbsp whole, unflavored psyllium husk

2 tsp baking powder

Directions: Preheat the oven to 350°F (175°C). Line a 6½ cup (1500 ml), round baking pan with parchment paper. Melt the butter and let it cool.

Beat the eggs for about 5 minutes until they're light and fluffy. Add in the cooled butter and the crème fraîche, and mix the batter thoroughly.

Mix all the dry ingredients together, and add them to the batter.

Pour the batter into the prepared pan, and bake on the middle rack for 35 to 40 minutes.

Test the sponge cake for doneness by inserting a toothpick in the center of the cake. The toothpick will come out dry if the cake is ready.

You can replace the vanilla flavor
with any of the following:
2 tsp ground cardamom
1½ tbsp ground cinnamon
1 small envelope of saffron
Grated rind and juice from 1 organic
orange or lemon
¼ cup (50 ml) cacao

Tosca Cake

Our Tosca cake baked following the LCHF guidelines will not turn out as crispy and toffee-like as the traditional Swedish Tosca baked with sugar. However, that doesn't mean ours doesn't taste wonderful. Go ahead and try it!

SERVES 8–10

CAKE

⅔ cup (150 g) unsalted butter

Oat fiber or coconut flour, for dusting

4 large eggs

½ cup (100 ml) crème fraîche or sour cream

2 tbsp erythritol/stevia blend (or other sweetener of your choice, see page 11)

¼ cup (50 ml) coconut flour

½ cup (100 ml) almond flour or ½ cup (50 g) ground almonds

1 heaping tbsp whole, unflavored psyllium husk

½ tsp vanilla powder or 1 tsp vanilla extract

2 tsp baking powder

TOSCA FROSTING

⅓ cup (75 g) unsalted butter

1 tbsp whipping cream

1½ tbsp erythritol/stevia blend (or other sweetener of your choice, see page 11)

⅛ tsp vanilla powder or ¼ tsp vanilla extract

1 tsp coconut flour

½ cup (50 g) slivered or chopped almonds

Directions: Preheat the oven to 350°F (175°C). Line the bottom of an 8½" (22 cm) springform pan with parchment paper, and butter and dust the sides with oat fiber or coconut flour. Melt and cool the butter.

Cake: Beat the eggs for 5 minutes, or until light and fluffy. Add in the cooled butter and the crème fraîche, and make sure they're thoroughly mixed.

Mix the dry ingredients together, and stir them into the batter.

Pour the batter into the prepared springform pan, and bake on the middle rack for 15 minutes. Remove the cake from the oven—DO NOT turn off the oven at this point, as the cake is not yet done baking.

Tosca frosting: Melt the butter in a heavy-bottomed saucepan. Add whipping cream, sweetener, vanilla powder, and coconut flour. Bring the mixture to a boil while you whisk. Let the mixture simmer until it has thickened. Mix in the slivered or chopped almonds.

Pour the frosting over the partly baked cake, and return it to the oven to continue cooking for about another 15 minutes. Let the cake cool, and then loosen it from the sides of the pan by running a sharp knife around the edge of the cake before opening the pan.

Almond Cake with Blueberry Topping

I love the taste of bitter almond, and in this cake the almond pairs up with blueberry to create a wonderful combination of flavors! I'm sure this cake will become a popular favorite!

SERVES 8–10

1¾ cup (400 ml) almond flour (or 2 cups (200 g) blanched, peeled, and ground almonds)

2 bitter almonds, ground (or 1 tsp almond extract)

2 tbsp erythritol/stevia blend (or other sweetener of your choice, see page 11)

4 large eggs, at room temperature

⅔ cup (150 g) unsalted butter, softened

¾ cup (150 ml) crème fraîche or sour cream

¼ cup (50 ml) coconut flour

1½ tsp baking powder

½ tsp vanilla powder or 1 tsp vanilla extract

½–1 cup (100–200 ml) fresh or frozen blueberries

½ cup (100 ml) slivered almonds

Oat fiber or coconut flour, for dusting the baking pan

Directions: Preheat the oven to 350°F (175°C). Line the bottom of an 8½" (22 cm) springform pan with parchment paper. Butter the sides, and dust them with oat fiber or coconut flour.

Place the almond flour, the ground bitter almonds, and sweetener in a food processor, and mix until everything is thoroughly blended.

Add in the eggs, one at a time, while keeping the machine running. Add in the softened butter and the crème fraîche, a little at a time, and continue processing until you end up with batter.

Mix all the dry ingredients together, and add them to the batter.

Spread the batter in the springform pan. Sprinkle the surface of the batter with blueberries and slivered almonds.

Bake the cake on the middle rack for approximately 30 minutes. Loosen the cake from the sides of the pan and let cool.

Dust the cake with a little erythritol/stevia blend (or other sweetener of your choice, see page 11) for a nice touch, right before serving.

Tip! Add an extra touch by serving the cake with custard sauce or lightly whipped cream.

Mazarin Cake

Almond and chocolate is a favorite blend of flavors, especially when used here in a Swedish classic dessert, the Mazarin cake. It's very filling, so a small piece goes a long way.

SERVES 8–10

CAKE

⅔ cup (150 g) unsalted butter
5 large eggs
½ cup (100 ml) whipping cream
1½ tbsp erythritol/stevia blend (or other sweetener of your choice, see page 11)
1 cup (200 ml) almond flour or 1 cup (100 g) ground almonds
4 bitter almonds, finely ground (or 2 tsp almond extract)
¼ cup (50 ml) coconut flour
2 tsp baking powder

CHOCOLATE GANACHE

½ cup (100 ml) whipping cream
1¾ oz (50 g) dark chocolate, 90% cacao
½ tbsp erythritol/stevia blend (or other sweetener of your choice, see page 11), optional

Directions: Preheat the oven to 350°F (175°C). Line the bottom of an 8½" (22 cm) springform pan with parchment paper. Melt the butter and let it cool.

Cake: Beat the eggs for about 5 minutes, or until they're light and fluffy. Add in the cooled butter and the whipping cream.

Mix all the dry ingredients together, and then mix them thoroughly into the batter.

Pour the batter into the springform pan and bake on the middle rack for approximately 25 minutes. Let the cake cool completely.

Chocolate ganache: Heat the cream in a saucepan. Remove the saucepan from the heat, and melt the chocolate in the cream while stirring. Add in the sweetener and mix thoroughly.

Refrigerate the ganache until it becomes spreadable. Spread the ganache over the cake, and store the cake in the refrigerator.

Strawberry Cake

I don't believe I'm exaggerating when I say that many of you will rely on this delicious treat for your coffee get-togethers in the future. The cake won't look fully baked as it comes out of the oven, but it will set nicely as it cools. You won't find a more delectable cake.

SERVES 8–10

CAKE

⅔ cup (150 g) unsalted butter, very soft

1 tbsp erythritol/stevia blend (or other sweetener of your choice, see page 11)

2 large eggs, at room temperature

½ cup (100 ml) coconut flour

1½ tsp baking powder

½ tsp vanilla powder or 1 tsp vanilla extract

FILLING

1 cup (200 ml) crème fraîche or sour cream

3 large eggs

½ tsp vanilla powder or 1 tsp vanilla extract

1 tbsp erythritol/stevia blend (or other sweetener of your choice, see page 11)

7 oz (200 g) fresh strawberries, sliced

Directions: Preheat the oven to 350°F (175°C). Line the bottom of an 8½" (22 cm) springform pan with parchment paper.

Cream the butter and sweetener until light and airy. Add in the eggs, one at a time, mixing thoroughly between each addition.

Mix the dry ingredients together thoroughly, and add them to the batter.

Pour the batter into the prepared springform pan.

Filling: Whip crème fraîche, eggs, vanilla powder, and sweetener until creamy. Pour the filling into the springform pan, and cover the top with sliced strawberries.

Bake on the middle rack for approximately 35 minutes.

Whipped cream and extra strawberries make scrumptious sides to the cake.

Blueberry Cupcakes

These lovely blueberry cupcakes are simply irresistible. Just make sure you don't eat all the topping before you've had a chance to decorate them.

SERVES 8–12

CUPCAKES

⅓ cup (75 g) unsalted butter

3 large eggs

½ cup (100 ml) crème fraîche or sour cream

2 tbsp erythritol/stevia blend (or other sweetener of your choice, see page 11)

½ tsp vanilla powder (or 1 tsp vanilla extract)

¼ cup (50 ml) coconut flour

¾ cup (150 ml) almond flour or ¾ cup (75 g) ground almonds

¼ cup (50 ml) hazelnut flour or ¾ cup (75 g) ground hazelnuts

1½ tsp baking powder

½ cup (100 ml) frozen or fresh blueberries

TOPPING

⅛ cup (25 ml) frozen blueberries

7 oz (200 g) cream cheese, at room temperature

1½ tbsp erythritol/stevia blend (or other sweetener of your choice, see page 11)

¼ cup (50 ml) whipping cream

Directions: Preheat the oven to 350°F (175°C). Melt the butter and let it cool.

Cupcakes: Beat the eggs for 5 minutes or until light and fluffy. Add in the cooled butter and the crème fraîche, and mix thoroughly.

Mix all the dry ingredients together thoroughly, and stir them into the batter. Carefully fold in the blueberries.

Line a muffin pan with baking cups and fill them with the mixture, using a spoon. Bake the cupcakes on the middle rack for approximately 15 to 20 minutes. Cool them on a baking rack.

Topping: Heat the blueberries to release their juice, then transfer them to a sieve and press them with a fork to collect all the juice.

Beat the cream cheese and sweetener until airy and light with a handheld electric mixer. Add in half the blueberry juice and check for color; the more juice you add to the mix, the richer the color. Add in the whipping cream; beat it until you have a creamy consistency without any lumps, and chill.

Pipe the topping in pretty patterns onto the cupcakes, and then refrigerate.

Rhubarb and Cinnamon Muffins

Substituting rhubarb for apples is common practice when baking according to LCHF guidelines; since the end result is these tasty muffins, you won't miss the apples.

SERVES 8–10

RHUBARB COMPÔTE
7–8¾ oz (200–250 g) rhubarb
⅛ cup (25 g) unsalted butter
1 tbsp erythritol/stevia blend (or other sweetener of your choice, see page 11)
2 tsp cinnamon, ground

MUFFINS
¼ cup (50 g) unsalted butter
5 large eggs
½ cup (100 ml) whipping cream
1½ tbsp erythritol/stevia blend (or other sweetener of your choice, see page 11)
½ cup (100 ml) coconut flour
½ cup (100 ml) almond flour or ½ cup (50 g) ground almonds
1½ tbsp whole, unflavored psyllium husk
2 tsp baking powder

Directions: Preheat the oven to 350°F (175°C). Melt the butter and let it cool.

Rhubarb compôte: Clean and chop the rhubarb into thin slices or smaller chunks. Fry the rhubarb gently in the butter until soft but without browning it. Sprinkle in the sweetener and cinnamon, and mix thoroughly. Let the fruit cool.

Muffins: Beat the eggs for 5 minutes or until they're light and fluffy. Add in the cooled butter and the whipping cream. Mix thoroughly.

Mix the dry ingredients together thoroughly, and stir them into the batter. Fold in the rhubarb compôte. Spoon the batter into muffin cups, and bake on the middle rack for approximately 15 to 20 minutes.

Tip! *Rhubarb compôte can also be used as a filling in the muffins. Fill half the muffin cup with batter, add a spoonful of compote, and add another dollop of batter to cover. If you prefer larger muffins, simply increase the baking time accordingly.*

Strawberry Cupcakes

These are truly summertime cupcakes—so go ahead and bake them for a midsummer party!

SERVES 10–12

CUPCAKES

⅓ cup (75 g) unsalted butter

5 large eggs

½ cup (100 ml) whipping cream

1½ tbsp erythritol/stevia blend (or
   other sweetener of your choice, see
   page 11)

½ cup (100 ml) coconut flour

½ cup (100 ml) almond flour or ½
   cup (50 g) ground almonds

1 tbsp whole, unflavored psyllium husk

½ tsp vanilla powder or 1 tsp vanilla
   extract

2 tsp baking powder

5¼ oz (150 g) fresh strawberries,
   coarsely chopped

TOPPING

⅔ cup (150 g) unsalted butter,
   softened

1 tbsp erythritol/stevia blend (or other
   sweetener of your choice, see page 11)

3½ oz (100 g) cream cheese, at room
   temperature

5¼ oz (150 g) fresh strawberries,
   finely chopped

GARNISH

Fresh strawberries

Directions: Preheat the oven to 350°F (175°C). Melt the butter and let it cool.

Cupcakes: Beat the eggs for 5 minutes or until they're light and fluffy. Add in the cooled butter and the whipping cream.

   Mix all the dry ingredients together, and incorporate them into the batter. Fold in the chopped strawberries. Spoon the batter into baking cups, preferably set into a muffin pan. Bake the cupcakes on the middle rack for approximately 15 to 20 minutes. Cool the cupcakes on a baking rack.

Topping: Cream the soft butter with the sweetener and cream cheese to a smooth consistency. Fold in the chopped strawberries and mix well. Pipe or place dollops of the topping onto the cooled cupcakes, and garnish them with strawberries. Refrigerate.

Chocolate Cupcakes with Raspberry Topping

I invented these cupcakes specifically for Father's Day a few years ago, but we've enjoyed them ever since at regular intervals during our coffee klatches, because they're absolutely fabulous!

SERVES 8–10

CUPCAKES

⅓ cup (75 g) unsalted butter

5 large eggs

½ cup (100 ml) whipping cream

2 tbsp erythritol/stevia blend (or other sweetener of your choice, see page 11)

⅓ cup (75 ml) coconut flour

2 tbsp whole, unflavored psyllium husk

¼ cup (50 ml) cacao

½ tsp vanilla powder or 1 tsp vanilla extract

2 tsp baking powder

RASPBERRY TOPPING

3½ oz (100 g) raspberries, frozen

7 oz (200 g) cream cheese

1½ tbsp erythritol/stevia blend (or other sweetener of your choice, see page 11)

¼ cup (50 ml) whipping cream

GARNISH

Fresh raspberries

Directions: Preheat the oven to 350°F (175°C). Melt the butter and let it cool.

Cupcakes: Beat the eggs for 5 minutes or until they're light and fluffy. Add in the cooled, melted butter and the whipping cream. Blend thoroughly.

Mix the dry ingredients together, and add them to the batter. Spoon the batter into baking cups, preferably set in a muffin pan. Bake on the middle rack for approximately 15 to 20 minutes. Let the cupcakes cool.

Raspberry topping: Heat up the raspberries until they release their juice, and then press them through a sieve to collect all their juice.

Beat the cream cheese and sweetener until creamy and with no lumps. Fold in the raspberry juice, and mix well. Add the whipping cream, a little at a time, and whip until the mix is light and airy.

Pipe or spread the topping onto the cupcakes, and garnish with fresh raspberries. Keep the cupcakes refrigerated.

Coconut Muffins with a Hidden Lime Surprise

Frozen muffins can be quickly defrosted and are the perfect treat to keep on hand in case you get a craving for something tasty!

SERVES 6–8

MUFFINS

⅓ cup (75 g) unsalted butter
4 large eggs
Juice of 1 organic lime
½ cup (100 ml) whipping cream
2 tbsp erythritol/stevia blend (or other sweetener of your choice, see page 11)
½ cup (100 ml) coconut flour
1 cup (200 ml) unsweetened, grated coconut
1 tbsp whole, unflavored psyllium husk
1½ tsp baking powder

LIME SURPRISE FILLING

½ cup (100 ml) cream cheese
Grated rind of 1 organic lime
½ tbsp erythritol/stevia blend (or other sweetener of your choice, see page 11)

GARNISH

Grated, unsweetened coconut

Directions: Preheat the oven to 350°F (175°C). Melt the butter and let it cool.

Lime surprise filling: Mix all ingredients thoroughly.

Beat the eggs for 5 minutes, or until light and fluffy. Add in the cooled butter, lime juice, and whipping cream.

Mix the dry ingredients together, and stir them into the batter.

With a spoon, fill the muffin cups three-quarters of the way, and make a small dent with the back of a wet spoon. Place a dollop of lime filling in the dent, and cover the filling with some more batter. Even out the batter on top so it covers the sides and closes up the filling. Sprinkle grated coconut over the tops of the muffins.

Bake the muffins on the middle rack for approximately 15 to 20 minutes.

Rhubarb and Cardamom Squares

Cardamom paired with rhubarb is one of the most enticing flavor combinations there is! Use the rhubarb's variegated red and green color to make a pretty pattern on the cake's surface.

SERVES 8–12

⅓ cup (100 g) unsalted butter

Oat fiber or coconut flour, for dusting

4 large eggs

2 tbsp erythritol/stevia blend (or other sweetener of your choice, see page 11)

1 cup (200 ml) whipping cream

¾ cup (150 ml) coconut flour

2½ tbsp whole, unflavored psyllium husk

1½ tsp baking powder

1 tsp cardamom, ground

Approx. 7 oz (200 g) rhubarb

Directions: Preheat the oven to 350°F (175°C). Melt the butter and let it cool. Butter a small baking pan, approx. 6" × 7¾" (15 × 20 cm) in size, and dust it with oat fiber or coconut flour.

Beat the eggs and sweetener for about 5 minutes, or until light and fluffy. Add in the whipping cream and the cooled butter. Mix well.

Mix the dry ingredients together, and stir them into the batter.

Spread the batter in the prepared baking pan, and bake on the middle rack for approximately 25 minutes.

Let the cake cool, and then cut it into squares. A dusting of erythritol/stevia blend (or other sweetener of your choice, see page 11) is always a nice addition. Serve the cake by itself or with a dollop of vanilla custard.

Coconut Squares

A snap to make, these coconut squares are just the ticket to accompany an afternoon cup.

SERVES 8–12

SPONGE CAKE

½ cup (100 g) unsalted butter

Oat fiber or coconut flour, for dusting

5 large eggs

2 tbsp erythritol/stevia blend (or other sweetener of your choice, see page 11)

1 cup (200 ml) whipping cream

¾ cup (150 ml) coconut flour

2 tbsp whole, unflavored psyllium husk

½ tsp vanilla powder or 1 tsp vanilla extract

2 tsp baking powder

COCONUT FROSTING

⅓ cup (75 g) unsalted butter

1 tbsp erythritol/stevia blend (or other sweetener of your choice, see page 11)

½ cup (100 ml) whipping cream

1½ cup (300 ml) grated, unsweetened coconut

1 large egg

Directions: Preheat the oven to 350°F (175°C). Melt the butter separately for the cake and the frosting, and let both cool. Butter a small baking pan, approx. 6" × 7¾" (15 × 20 cm) in size, and dust it with oat fiber or coconut flour.

Sponge cake: Beat the eggs for about 5 minutes, or until light and fluffy. Add in the cooled butter and the whipping cream. Mix thoroughly.

Mix the dry ingredients together, and mix into the batter.

Spread the batter in the prepared baking pan, and bake on the middle rack for approximately 15 minutes. Remove the cake (which is only partly baked at this stage) from the oven, and leave the oven on.

Coconut frosting: Add sweetener, whipping cream, and grated coconut to the cooled butter. Mix everything thoroughly into the butter. Stir in the egg.

Spread the frosting over the cake, and return the cake to the oven to continue baking for another 10 minutes or so.

Coconut and Chocolate Squares

You really can't beat the combination of coconut and chocolate—
think of the candy bar, Mounds, and you'll get an idea of how
sensational these squares taste!

SERVES 8–12

CAKE

½ cup (100 g) unsalted butter
5 large eggs
½ cup (100 ml) mascarpone
2 tbsp erythritol/stevia blend (or other
  sweetener of your choice, see page 11)
¼ cup (50 ml) cacao
½ cup (100 ml) almond flour or ½
  cup (50 g) ground almonds
¼ cup (50 ml) coconut flour
2 tbsp whole, unflavored psyllium husk
½ tsp vanilla powder or 1 tsp vanilla
  extract
2 tsp baking powder
Oat fiber or coconut flour for dusting
  the pan

COCONUT BUTTERCREAM

¾ cup (175 g) unsalted butter
1½ tbsp erythritol/stevia blend (or
  other sweetener of your choice, see
  page 11)
2 large eggs
3 cups (250 g) unsweetened coconut,
  grated

CHOCOLATE GANACHE

3½ oz (100 g) dark chocolate, 90%
  cacao
½ cup (100 ml) whipping cream
¼ tsp vanilla powder or ½ tsp vanilla
  extract
½ tbsp erythritol/stevia blend (or other
  sweetener of your choice, see page
  11), optional

Directions: Preheat the oven to 350°F
(175°C). Melt the butter and let it cool.
Butter a small baking pan, approx. 6" × 9¾"
(15 × 25 cm) in size, and dust it with oat
fiber or coconut flour.

Cake: Beat the eggs for about 5 minutes,
or until light and fluffy. Add in the cooled
butter, and then the mascarpone and the
sweetener.

Mix all the dry ingredients together and
stir them into the batter. Pour the batter
into the prepared baking pan.

Bake on the middle rack for approximately
25 minutes. Let the cake cool completely.

Coconut buttercream: Melt butter and sweetener together, and let cool. Add in the eggs
and the grated coconut, and stir to blend
thoroughly. Spread the buttercream over the
cake and refrigerate.

Chocolate ganache: Coarsely chop the chocolate. Heat the whipping cream, and then
remove the saucepan from the heat. Add
the chopped chocolate, vanilla powder, and
sweetener (if using) to the warm cream, and
stir thoroughly to make the chocolate melt.
Let it cool.

Spread the chocolate ganache on top of
the coconut buttercream, and put the cake
back in the refrigerator.

Orange Squares

"Ambrosia cake" is a Swedish classic and a favorite at many a coffee break gathering. Here is our LCHF version!

SERVES 8–12

CAKE

½ cup (100 g) unsalted butter

Oat fiber or coconut flour, for dusting

5 large eggs

2 tbsp erythritol/stevia blend (or other sweetener of your choice, see page 11)

Grated rind and juice from 1 organic orange

1 cup (200 ml) whipping cream

½ cup (100 ml) coconut flour

½ cup (100 ml) almond flour or ½ cup (50 g) ground almonds

2 tbsp whole, unflavored psyllium husk

2 tsp baking powder

ORANGE FROSTING

5¼ oz (150 g) cream cheese, at room temperature

1½ tbsp erythritol/stevia blend (or other sweetener of your choice, see page 11)

⅔ cup (150 g) unsalted butter

Grated rind from 1 organic orange

GARNISH

Grated rind from 1 organic orange

Directions: Preheat the oven to 350°F (175°C). Melt the butter and let it cool. Grease a small baking pan, approx. 6" × 9¾" (15 × 25 cm) in size, and dust it with oat fiber or coconut flour.

Cake: Beat the eggs for 5 minutes, or until they're light and fluffy. Add in the melted butter, orange juice, grated rind, and whipping cream. Mix thoroughly.

Mix all the dry ingredients together and add them to the batter. Pour the batter into the prepared baking pan, and bake on the middle rack for approximately 30 minutes. Let the cake cool completely.

Orange frosting: Whip the cream cheese, sweetener, and butter until creamy and without any lumps. Add in the grated orange rind and stir well.

Spread the frosting over the cooled cake; use a dry, warm knife if you want a smooth surface.

A little grated orange rind makes for a pretty finish when sprinkled onto the frosting.

Buns and Pastries

Cinnamon Buns

I'm immensely proud of my cinnamon bun recipe! There are many recipes for LCHF cinnamon buns out there these days, but in the beginning there was only one—this one! Now you too can bake these treats from the original recipe!

SERVES 10–12

DOUGH

⅓ cup (50 g) unsalted butter

4 large eggs + 1 yolk

2 tbsp erythritol/stevia blend (or other sweetener of your own choice, see page 11)

½ cup (100 ml) whipping cream

1 tsp ground cardamom

¾ cup (150 ml) coconut flour

3 tbsp whole, unflavored psyllium husk

2 tsp baking powder

FILLING

¼ cup (50 g) unsalted butter, softened

1½–2 tbsp ground cinnamon

½ tbsp erythritol/stevia blend (or other sweetener of your own choice, see page 11)

GARNISH

1 whipped egg white, for glazing

Chopped almonds

Directions: Preheat the oven to 350°F (175°C). Melt the butter and let it cool.

Beat the eggs, yolk, and sweetener for 5 minutes, or until light and fluffy.

Add the whipping cream and the melted, cool butter, and mix thoroughly.

Mix all the dry ingredients together, and incorporate them into the batter to make dough. Let the dough rest for at least 5 minutes.

Roll out the dough between two greased sheets of parchment paper, and then remove the top sheet.

Spread the softened butter over the entire surface of the dough, and give it a liberal sprinkling of ground cinnamon. Roll up the dough as if making a Swiss roll. Slice the roll of dough into individual buns and set them in muffin tins.

Glaze the buns with beaten egg white, and sprinkle the tops with chopped almonds.

Bake the buns on the middle rack of the oven for approximately 15 minutes.

HEADS UP! *The butter will melt while baking, but will be absorbed by the buns as they cool.*

Tip! *The Pistachio Buns can also be baked as a flat loaf.*

Pistachio Buns

Pistachio nuts are a favorite in our family, and so are these buns! They're at their best the day after baking, as their flavor will have had a time to fully blossom.

SERVES **10–12**

DOUGH

¼ cup (50 g) unsalted butter

4 large eggs + 1 yolk

½ cup (100 ml) whipping cream

2 tbsp erythritol/stevia blend (or other sweetener of your choice, see page 11)

½ cup (100 ml) coconut flour

½ cup (100 ml) pistachio nuts, ground

3 tbsp whole, unflavored psyllium husk

½ tsp vanilla powder or 1 tsp vanilla extract

2 tsp baking powder

FILLING

1 cup (200 ml) pistachio nuts, ground

½ cup (100 g) unsalted butter, softened

1 tbsp erythritol/stevia blend (or other sweetener of your choice, see page 11)

GARNISH

1 beaten egg white for glazing

Pistachio nuts, chopped

Directions: Preheat oven to 350°F (175°C). Melt the butter and let it cool. Line a baking sheet with parchment paper.

Filling: Mix all ingredients to make a smooth filling.

Dough: Beat the eggs and the yolk until light and fluffy, at least 5 minutes. Add the whipping cream and the cooled butter. Mix thoroughly.

Mix the dry ingredients together, and add them to the batter to make dough. Let the dough rest for at least 5 minutes.

Roll the dough into a rectangle measuring about 6" × 10" (15 × 25 cm) between two sheets of greased parchment paper. Remove the top sheet of parchment paper. Spread the filling over the entire surface of the dough. Fold the long sides of the dough toward the middle so their edges meet, then fold them once again lengthwise to make a long tube of dough that is 4 layers thick.

Slice the dough into 10 to 12 buns, and place them on the prepared baking sheet. Brush the buns with the beaten egg white, and sprinkle them with chopped pistachio nuts.

Bake the buns on the middle rack of the oven for approximately 15 to 20 minutes.

Swedish Saffron Buns

*During the 2011 Christmas season, I introduced this innovative LCHF alternative
to a traditional Swedish saffron bun, served traditionally on St. Lucia's Day, and like
the cinnamon buns, they were an instant hit! Traditions are cozy and comforting, so
why not start a new one this year?*

SERVES 10–12

DOUGH

¼ cup (50 g) unsalted butter
4 large eggs + 1 yolk
1 packet saffron
⅓ cup (100 ml) whipping cream
2 tbsp erythritol/stevia blend (or other
  sweetener of your choice, see page 11)
½ cup (100 ml) coconut flour
3 tbsp whole, unflavored psyllium husk
2 tsp baking powder

GARNISH

1 beaten egg white, for glazing
Raisins (optional)

Directions: Preheat the oven to 350°F
(175°C). Melt the butter and let it cool.
Line a baking sheet with parchment
paper.

Beat the eggs and the yolk for 5 minutes, or until light and fluffy. Add in the
cooled butter, saffron powder, and whipping cream, and mix thoroughly.

Mix the dry ingredients together, and
stir them into the batter to make dough.
Let the dough rest for at least 5 minutes.

Roll out 10 narrow lengths of dough
and make them into the proper shape by
turning in the ends to form a closed "S";
turn one end to the right, the other to
the left.

Set the buns on the prepared baking
sheet and brush them with the egg white
glaze.

Bake the buns on the middle rack of
the oven for approximately 15 minutes.

Tip! *Raisins are not LCHF, so it's up to you if you want to include raisins in these buns or not.*

Tip! *If you choose to use another type of nut, this cake will still be delectable!*

Pecan Pastry

This cake brings to mind the most delicious of Danish pastries—the pecan Danish. Don't say I didn't warn you—it is difficult to stop eating this once you've had a taste. . . .

SERVES 10–12

PASTRY

2⅛ tbsp (30 g) unsalted butter
3 large eggs
¼ cup (50 ml) whipping cream
1½ tbsp erythritol/stevia blend (or other sweetener of your choice, see page 11)
⅓ cup (75 ml) coconut flour
1½ tbsp whole, unflavored psyllium husk
½ tsp vanilla powder or 1 tsp vanilla extract
1½ tsp baking powder

PECAN FILLING

⅓ cup (75 g) unsalted butter
1 tbsp whipping cream
1½ tbsp erythritol/stevia blend (or other sweetener of your choice, see page 11)
1 tsp coconut flour
2½ oz (75 g) pecans, coarsely chopped (rinsed and dried if they're salted)

Directions: Preheat the oven to 350°F (175°C). Melt the butter and let it cool. Line a baking sheet with parchment paper.

Pastry layer: Beat the eggs for 5 minutes, or until light and fluffy. Add in the whipping cream and the cooled butter, and mix thoroughly.

Mix the dry ingredients together, and incorporate them in the batter to make dough. Let it rest for at least 5 minutes or until you can work the dough.

With slightly wet hands, shape the dough into a long piece, about 4" × 10" (10 × 25 cm). Make an edge all around to contain the filling.

Place the pastry layer on the prepared baking sheet.

Pecan filling: Melt the butter, and add in the other ingredients save for the pecans. Let the mixture simmer while whisking it until it thickens slightly. Stir in the chopped nuts.

Pour the filling onto the layer of cake, while making sure it doesn't flow over the edge.

Bake the cake on the middle rack of the oven for approximately 20 minutes. Let it cool completely on the baking sheet covered by a kitchen towel.

Cookies
and Tartlets

Orange Cookies

This is one heavenly cookie! And you'll be satisfied with a cup of coffee and just one of these treats, due to their powerful, heady taste of orange and chocolate.

MAKES 12–15 COOKIES

3 large eggs, at room temperature
½ cup (100 g) unsalted butter,
    softened
Grated rind from 1 organic orange
1½ tbsp erythritol/stevia blend (or
    other sweetener of your choice, see
    page 11)
½ cup (100 ml) coconut flour
¾ cup (150 ml) almond flour or ¾
    cup (75 g) ground almonds
½ tsp vanilla powder or 1 tsp vanilla
    extract
1 tsp baking powder

GARNISH

1¾ oz (50 g) melted chocolate, 90%
cacao

Directions: Preheat the oven to 350°F (175°C). Line a cookie sheet with parchment paper.

Cream one egg at a time with the very soft butter, and add in the grated orange peel.

Mix the dry ingredients together, and incorporate them into the batter to make dough.

Roll the dough into a thick cylinder, about 1¼" to 2" (3–5 cm) in diameter and about 6" to 8" (15–20 cm) long. Refrigerate the dough for at least 30 minutes.

Cut the dough into ½" (1 cm) slices, and set them quite closely together on the prepared cookie sheet.

Bake the cookies on the middle rack for approximately 10 to 15 minutes.

Let the cookies cool completely on a baking rack under a dishtowel.

Drizzle coils of melted chocolate onto the cookies, and let the chocolate set.

Chess Squares

These classic cookies are always a welcome part of the coffee break. They will not bake as crispy as cookies made with sugar, but they'll still taste wonderful!

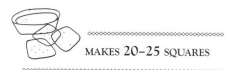

MAKES **20–25** SQUARES

LIGHT DOUGH

½ cup (100 g) unsalted butter

1½ tbsp erythritol/stevia blend (or
  other sweetener of your choice, see
  page 11)

3 large eggs, at room temperature

¾ cup (150 ml) coconut flour

½ tsp vanilla powder or 1 tsp vanilla
  extract

1 tsp baking powder

DARK DOUGH

½ cup (100 g) unsalted butter

1½ tbsp erythritol/stevia blend (or
  other sweetener of your choice, see
  page 11)

3 large eggs, at room temperature

¾ cup (150 ml) coconut flour

¼ cup (50 ml) cacao

½ tsp vanilla powder or 1 tsp vanilla
  extract

1 tsp baking powder

Directions: Preheat oven to 350°F (175°C). Line a cookie sheet with parchment paper.

Prepare the two types of dough separately, in two bowls.

Cream the butter with the sweetener. Add in the eggs, one at a time.

Mix all the dry ingredients and stir them into the batter to make dough. Let the dough rest for a few minutes.

Separate each color into two evenly sized pieces, and roll them into lengths. Place one light and one dark piece of dough side by side. Then place one light length of dough on top of a dark length of dough, and one dark length of dough on top of the remaining light length of dough. Press down on the dough to form a thick square, approximately 9" to 11¾" (25–30 cm) in length. Let the dough rest in the refrigerator for about 30 minutes.

Cut the dough into ½" slices, and place them quite closely together on the prepared cookie sheet. Even out the edges to make square-shaped cookies.

Bake the cookies on the oven's middle rack for about 10 to 15 minutes.

Hazelnut Cookies

These are the simplest cookies of them all, but perhaps also the tastiest, especially if you love hazelnuts! LCHF cooking or baking sometimes makes for a lot of leftover egg whites, and this recipe is the perfect opportunity to use them up!

MAKES 15–20 COOKIES

1 cup (200 ml) hazelnuts
2 egg whites
1½ tbsp erythritol/stevia blend (or other sweetener of your choice, see page 11)

GARNISH
15–20 hazelnuts

Directions: Preheat the oven to 350°F (175°C). Line a cookie sheet with parchment paper.

Grind the hazelnuts in a small grinder. Beat the egg whites until stiff peaks form—if you tip the bowl upside down, the whites should stay in place. Fold in the nuts and the sweetener.

Spoon 15 to 20 cookies onto the prepared cookie sheet and place a hazelnut on each cookie.

Bake the cookies on the oven's middle rack for approximately 15 minutes.

Imperial Crowns

The old Swedish name for these tartlets is Kongresser. They're true classics that still proudly have a place on our coffee tables today.

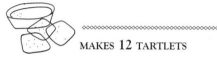

MAKES 12 TARTLETS

SHORT CRUST PASTRY

1 cup (120 g) unsalted butter

1 large egg + 4 yolks

1½ tbsp erythritol/stevia blend (or other sweetener of your choice, see page 11)

½ tsp vanilla powder or 1 tsp vanilla extract

¾ cup (150 ml) coconut flour

½ cup (100 ml) almond flour or ½ cup (50 g) ground almonds

1 tbsp whole psyllium husk, unflavored

1½ tsp baking powder

FILLING

4 egg whites

1 tbsp erythritol/stevia blend (or other sweetener of your choice, see page 11)

1½ cup (300 ml) hazelnut flour or 1 ½ cup (150 g) ground hazelnuts

Directions: Preheat the oven to 350°F (175°C). Melt the butter and let it cool.

Short crust pastry: Beat the eggs and yolks until light and fluffy; add in the cool, melted butter; and mix thoroughly.

Mix the dry ingredients together, and incorporate them into the batter to make pastry dough. Let the pastry rest for 5 minutes.

Roll out the dough and cut out 24 small, slim strips (use about ¼ of the total dough) to be placed in a lattice pattern on the tartlets. Place the rest of the dough in 12 fluted Mazarin tartlet molds, pressing the dough all the way up the sides.

Filling: Lightly whisk the egg whites, adding in the sweetener and the flour or nuts.

Fill the pastry-lined molds with the filling; add the lattice top, using the thin strips of dough, on top of the filling.

Bake on the oven's middle rack for approximately 15 minutes. Let cool.

If desired, dust the tartlets with a bit of erythritol/stevia blend (or other sweetener of your choice, see page 11) right before serving.

Coconut and Raspberry Mazarin Tartlets

A bright, summery flavor that's just right for a coffee table nestled in a lilac-covered arbor. Or enjoy them in the middle of winter, when you long to recapture some summer memories.

MAKES **12** TARTLETS

SHORT CRUST PASTRY

½ cup (125 g) unsalted butter

2 large eggs

1½ tbsp erythritol/stevia blend (or other sweetener of your choice, see page 11)

½ tsp vanilla powder (or 1 tsp vanilla extract)

¾ cup (150 ml) coconut flour

1½ tsp baking powder

FILLING

7 tbsp (100 g) unsalted butter

2 large eggs

1 cup (200 ml) grated, unsweetened coconut

1 tbsp erythritol/stevia blend (or other sweetener of your choice, see page 11)

1 cup (200 ml) fresh or frozen raspberries

Directions: Preheat the oven to 350°F (175°C). Melt the butter for the pastry, and let it cool. Melt butter for the filling, and let it cool.

Short crust pastry: Beat the eggs and sweetener until light and fluffy; add in the cool, melted butter and mix thoroughly.

Mix the dry ingredients together, and incorporate them into the batter to make pastry dough. Let the pastry rest for 5 minutes.

Divide the pastry into 12 pieces; line the Mazarin tartlet molds with the pastry and press it all the way up the sides.

Filling: Beat the eggs and add in the cool, melted butter. Stir in the grated coconut, sweetener, and raspberries.

Add filling to each of the 12 pastry-lined molds.

Bake the tartlets on the oven's middle rack for approximately 15 minutes.

Tip! You can make one large tart instead of individual tartlets!

Tip! *The unbaked, unfilled pastry shells can be frozen.*

Chocolate Mazarin Tartlets with Ganache and Tosca Topping

A burst of chocolate on your taste buds! These tartlets are perfect when paired with a cup of strong coffee.

MAKES 10–12 TARTLETS

SHORT CRUST PASTRY
½ cup (125 g) unsalted butter
2 large eggs
1½ tbsp erythritol/stevia blend (or other sweetener of your choice, see page 11)
½ cup (100 ml) coconut flour
¼ cup (50 ml) cacao powder
1½ tsp baking powder
½ tsp vanilla powder or 1 tsp vanilla extract

MAZARIN FILLING
1 large egg
1 tbsp erythritol/stevia blend (or other sweetener of your choice, see page 11)
1 tbsp cacao powder
½ cup (50 g) blanched, peeled, and ground almonds
1 small bitter almond, ground, or ½ tsp almond extract
1¾ oz or ¼ cup (50 g) unsalted butter, very soft

GANACHE FILLING
1¾ oz (50 g) dark chocolate, 90% cacao
⅓ cup (75 ml) whipping cream
½ tbsp erythritol/stevia blend (or other sweetener of your choice, see page 11)

TOSCA TOPPING
3½ oz (100 g) hazelnuts
3½ oz (100 g) almonds
1¾ oz (50 g) unsalted butter
1½ tbsp erythritol/stevia blend (or other sweetener of your choice, see page 11)
1 tsp coconut flour
½ tbsp whipping cream

Ganache filling: To be made a day in advance.

Coarsely chop the chocolate. Heat the whipping cream in a saucepan. Remove the saucepan from the heat and whisk in the chocolate and sweetener. Chill overnight.

Directions: Toast the hazelnuts and almonds in a 400°F (200°C) oven for 8 to 10 minutes. Remove the hazelnuts and almonds, and let them cool before coarsely chopping them.

Lower the oven temperature to 350°F (175°C). Melt the butter for the pastry, and let it cool.

Short crust pastry: Beat the eggs and sweetener until light and fluffy. Add the cool, melted butter. Mix the dry ingredients thoroughly, and incorporate them into the batter to make pastry dough. Let the pastry rest for 5 minutes.

Divide the pastry dough between 10 to 12 round Mazarin molds, and press the dough all the way up the sides.

Mazarin filling: Beat the egg with the sweetener and cacao powder. Stir in the ground almonds and bitter almond. Add in the butter a little at a time, and beat until it becomes a smooth batter. Pour the filling into the pastry-lined molds.

Bake the tartlets on the middle rack for approximately 12 minutes. Let the tartlets cool completely.

Tosca topping: Bring the butter, sweetener, coconut flour, and whipping cream to a boil, while whisking. Let the mixture simmer until it thickens. Stir in the chopped hazelnuts and almonds. Let the Tosca topping cool completely.

Spread the chocolate ganache over the tartlets, and add a dollop of the Tosca topping onto each tartlet. Keep refrigerated.

Peanut Tartlets

Consider this a fair warning: These tartlets are so tempting that it's easy to overindulge!

MAKES 12–14 TARTLETS

TARTLET CRUST

½ cup (125 g) unsalted butter

2 large eggs

1½ tbsp erythritol/stevia blend (or other sweetener of your choice, see page 11)

½ tsp vanilla powder or 1 tsp vanilla extract

¼ cup (50 ml) smooth, unsweetened peanut butter

¾ cup (150 ml) coconut flour

1½ tsp baking powder

FILLING

1¾ oz (50 g) dark chocolate, 90% cacao

1 egg yolk

2 tbsp smooth, unsweetened peanut butter

1 tbsp erythritol/stevia blend (or other sweetener of your choice, see page 11)

¼ tsp vanilla powder (or ½ tsp vanilla extract)

¾ cup (150 ml) whipping cream

GARNISH

Whole or coarsely chopped peanuts

Directions: Preheat the oven to 350°F (175°C). Melt the butter and let it cool.

Beat the eggs until light and fluffy, approximately 5 minutes. Add in the cooled butter, sweetener, vanilla powder, and peanut butter. Mix thoroughly.

Mix the coconut flour with the baking powder, and add it to the batter to make dough. Let the dough rest for 5 minutes.

Divide the dough between 12 to 14 round Mazarin tartlet molds, and press the dough all the way up the sides.

Bake the tartlets on the oven's middle rack for about 10 minutes. Let the tartlets cool completely before filling them. They can also be frozen at this stage (before filling).

Filling: In a bowl over hot water (bain-marie) melt the chocolate, while stirring. Remove the bowl from the heat and let chocolate cool slightly before stirring in the egg yolk. Add the peanut butter, sweetener, and vanilla powder, and stir thoroughly. Whip the cream and fold it carefully into the chocolate batter.

Fill the tartlets with the peanut filling, and sprinkle coarsely chopped or whole peanuts on top. Refrigerate for a few hours before serving.

Index

My heartfelt thanks:

To ICA Book Publishing and to Maria, because you decided to publish my third baking book!

To everybody who has been involved with this book in any and all ways!

To all my dear friends and family, and to Iittala's Outlet Store in Borås, Sweden (especially Emelie) for so graciously lending me wonderful place settings and tablecloths to make the book's photographs extra pretty. It couldn't have been done without you!

To my wonderful children, Magnus, Peter, and Elisabeth, and to my family, relatives, and wonderful friends for never tiring of testing my new recipes and providing me with constructive comments—getting so much honest feedback from so many taste buds has been absolutely invaluable!

And last but not least, to my wonderful husband, Mikael, who is always supportive, even when things are at their most hectic!

Visit my blog at www.mariannslchf.se, and www.mariannlchf.com to find more recipes and information about LCHF.

SteviaVital®Bakery+: *www.steviavital.se*
Aman Prana coconut flour and other LCHF products: *www.bodystore.com, www.lchfbutiken.se, www.skipper.smart.se*

English Translation © 2015 by Skyhorse Publishing
First published in 2014 as *Kakor och Desserter med LCHF* by Mariann Andersson,
Bonnier Fakta, Sweden
Photography: Martin Skredsvik
Graphics and cover: Lina Bergström

Skyhorse Publishing books may be purchased in bulk at special discounts for sales promotion, corporate gifts, fund-raising, or educational purposes. Special editions can also be created to specifications. For details, contact the Special Sales Department, Skyhorse Publishing, 307 West 36th Street, 11th Floor, New York, NY 10018 or info@skyhorsepublishing.com.

Skyhorse® and Skyhorse Publishing® are registered trademarks of Skyhorse Publishing, Inc.®, a Delaware corporation. www.skyhorsepublishing.com
10 9 8 7 6 5 4 3 2 1
Library of Congress Cataloging-in-Publication Data is available on file.

Print ISBN: 978-1-63450-397-6
Ebook ISBN: 978-1-63450-879-7

Printed in China